The Journey That Saved *Curious George*

The True Wartime Escape *of* Margret and H. A. Rey

By bicycle.... and train through FRANCE, SPAIN, and PORTUGAL

ATLANTIC OCEAN

PARIS

Étampes
Acquebouille
Orléans

FRANCE

Avranches

Bordeaux

château Feuga

Biarritz
Bayonne
Hendaye

PORTUGAL

SPAIN

Fuentes de Oñoro

Lisbon

Leaving Paris

Étampes

Through Spain

Portugal

For
Amy Flynn, Emily Linsay, and Eleni Beja…
my fine editors who shared the journey with me…

for
Lay Lee Ong…

and always,
for Pete.
— L.B.

For Louise, who made the journey.
— A.D.

❦

Acknowledgments

The names on the list of people who helped me unlock the past and the Reys' wartime experiences are many. Early encouragers were my husband, Pete, Susan Stark, Johanna Hurwitz, and Camilla Warrick. Lay Lee Ong, the executor of the Rey estate, strongly cheered me on. So did Cate, Ayars, and Ted Borden, and colleagues in the children's book world: M. K. Kroeger, Cat Smith, Margaret McElderry, Emma Dryden, Ann Bobco, George Ella Lyon, Barb Libby, and Connie Trounstine.

Additional thanks go to the following friends:

The de Grummond Collection: Dee Jones, Ann Ashmore, Ginamarie Pugliese, and Danielle Bishop
Houghton Mifflin: Eden Edwards, Sheila Smallwood, Carol Goldenberg Rosen, Andrea Pinkney, Judy O'Malley
French and German translations: Renée Lowther, Cindy Curchin, Kurt Stark, and David Hunter
Conversations about the Reys: In the United States: Lay Lee Ong, André Schiffrin, Grace Maccarone, Charlotte Zolotow, Lee Bennett Hopkins, Marc Simont, and Leonard Marcus; in London: Pat Schleger
Terrass Hotel: Jean Max Hurand and Jean Luc Binet, whose family has owned and managed the hotel since 1912
Château Feuga: Shelagh and Christopher Stedman, of London and St. Mézard, France, who are the current owners of the château, and Christine Reon, of Lectoure, France
Travels, train routes, and maps: Mary Ann Iemmola
Montmartre, Étampes, Acquebouille, Orléans, Agen, Lectoure, St. Mézard, Castex-Lectourois, Château Feuga: Patty Hegman
Avranches: Cindy Curchin and Fr. Tobie, Abbaye du Mont-Saint-Michel
Hamburg and the Hagenbeck Zoo: Klaus Gille
Consulates and train stations in Biarritz, Bayonne, and Hendaye: Pete Borden and Elena Pérez

I would also like to thank Allan Drummond for his wonderful illustrations, and for understanding the vision for this book. Hans and Margret Rey would be very pleased by Allan's fine artistic talent and creative imagination.

The Journey That Saved Curious George

The True Wartime Escape *of* Margret and H. A. Rey

by Louise Borden   Illustrated *by* Allan Drummond

HOUGHTON MIFFLIN HARCOURT ★ BOSTON   NEW YORK

Finding the Story

For many years, I was intrigued by the story of Margret and H. A. Rey's flight from Paris on bicycles in June 1940. Others in the children's book field had mentioned this escape from the Nazi invasion, but no one seemed to know the details of those harrowing days. The story felt incomplete. I wanted to know more. I wanted real images. I was *curious*, just like the Reys' famous little monkey, George.

And so I began my own journey, a journey of research. A rich source for my research was Margret and Hans Rey's personal papers, donated by their estate to the de Grummond Children's Literature Collection at the University of Southern Mississippi. This nationally known library houses the papers and original artwork of more than 1,200 children's book authors and illustrators.

But after sifting through hundreds of the Reys' letters, notebook pages, and photographs, and even after walking through Paris on various research trips, I still had questions without answers. How many kilometers did the Reys travel on those two bicycles? Which roads did they follow on their journey south? What happened to the belongings that they had to leave behind? What wartime dangers did they face?

Over several years I had conversations in person or by phone with people who had known the Reys. I wrote letters and e-mailed people in Germany, England, Portugal, and France. And I traveled to some of the towns, cities, and addresses gleaned from the letters and work diaries that the Reys wrote during 1936–40, the years that they lived in Paris. Each step of the way, I tried to focus on Margret and Hans before *Curious George* was published and brought them fame.

Dates, postmarks, travel papers, and expense records provided invaluable clues in French, English, German, and Portuguese. Newspaper interviews from the 1940s and 1950s gave me needed details. Slowly, piece by piece, I began to stitch together the fabric of their story.

The Journey That Saved Curious George is my way, as a writer, of becoming a witness to part of Hans and Margret Rey's story. It is my way of honoring their creativity and their courage during a dark time in history for many countries of Europe.

Louise Borden

Above: H. A. and Margret Rey at a book signing, ca. 1945
Opposite, left: H. A. Rey, born September 16, 1898
Opposite, right: Margret Rey, born May 16, 1906

Two Artists

PART I

Childhoods in Germany

In 1906,
Hans Augusto Reyersbach
was a boy growing up in Hamburg, Germany,
a port city with canals and a thousand bridges . . .
and the River Elbe that ran to the North Sea.

At the age of eight,
Hans spent many hours in the cold breeze near Hamburg's docks,
watching foreign ships and barges move along the Elbe.
For the rest of his life,
Hans would love boats and rivers and the sea.

1906

Often Hans visited the Hagenbeck Zoo
with his brother and two sisters.
Monkeys and lions! Polar bears and seals!
The world of animals from faraway places
was just a few streets from the Reyersbach home.

It was at this wonderful zoo
that Hans learned to imitate the sounds of animals.
He could roar like a fierce lion.
He could bark like a seal.
Another favorite place for young Hans was the circus.
All those horses and bright colors!
What a show!

Hans loved to draw pictures and paint.
And he was good at it.
Hans made a painting of horses in the park,
near one of Hamburg's beautiful lakes.
Later, in school,
Hans studied Latin and Greek,
French and English.
He knew five languages, including German.

Left: *Scenes of Hamburg at the beginning of the twentieth century*
Top right: *Illustration by H.A. Rey in* Whiteblack the Penguin, *2000*
Bottom right: *Painting by Hans Reyersbach, 1906*

Margarete Waldstein,
who was born the same year that Hans turned eight,
also grew up in Hamburg during those early years of a new century.
Like the Reyersbach family,
the Waldsteins were Jewish.
Margarete and her two brothers and two sisters
had a good life,
full of comfort
and culture
and books.
Margarete wanted to become an artist.
Later she studied art and photography
at a school in Germany:
the famous Bauhaus.

Street in Hamburg at the turn of the nineteenth century

Klosterschule

Zeugnis der Reife.

Fräulein Margarethe Elisabeth Waldstein

Top left: *Margarete Waldstein as a toddler*
Top right: *Margarete Waldstein as a young girl*
Bottom: *Margret's certificate of completion for Klosterschule.*
Official documents show different spellings of her first name.

The next years were full of change and adventure
for Hans Reyersbach.
During World War I,
he was a soldier in Kaiser Wilhelm's German army.
Hans didn't like war, and he didn't like being a soldier.
And he was still drawing pictures.
Hans loved to laugh,
so sometimes his sketches were quite funny.

On clear nights,
he studied the stars and the constellations.
Hans was a deep thinker as well as an artist.
Always, he was *curious* about the world.
Because of his months on the eastern front,
Hans could now speak a smattering of Russian.

Above: *Hans Reyersbach as a young German soldier*
Opposite, top: *Sketches by Hans Reyersbach*

When Germany lost the war,
twenty-year-old Hans Reyersbach went home to Hamburg
and found work making posters for the local circus.
But times were very hard in his city,
and there was little money.
After a few years as a university student,
Hans packed his sketchbooks,
his paintbrushes,
and his pipe
and headed to Brazil on a ship.

Teaming Up in Brazil

In 1924,
Rio de Janeiro was an exotic city
  with tall, rugged mountains on one side
  and the blue sea on the other.
   It was a great port of world trade, like Hamburg.
   Its plazas and streets were swirls of colored tiles.
   Hans liked to stroll along Copacabana,
  a wide beach with crowds of bathers
and rows of striped umbrellas and tents.
It was *hot* in Brazil—
so Hans wore a broad hat,
even in the shade of Rio's palm trees and cafés.

1924

Top left: *Photograph of a Rio beach by Margarete Waldstein*
Illustrations: *From Curious George, 1941*
Bottom right: *Poster of Brazilian coffee markets by H. A. Rey*

When he traveled up and down the Amazon River,
Hans watched the monkeys and made drawings of them.
Monkeys and more monkeys!
And they weren't in a zoo.
They chattered in the branches of trees
in the small towns where Hans traveled
as he sold bathtubs and kitchen sinks to earn money.
Now he was fluent in another language:
Portuguese.

Nine years after Hans left Hamburg,
Adolf Hitler came to power in Germany.
Life began to change for the German people,
especially for Germans who were Jewish.
Margarete Waldstein left Hamburg
and worked as a photographer in London.
Then in 1935,
as Hans had done years earlier,
Margarete traveled the long ocean miles
to Rio de Janeiro.
She was looking for new work and adventure,
and she knew that Hans Reyersbach,
an old family friend whom she admired,
was living in Rio.

The two artists began to work together in business,
sharing their talents in writing and drawing.
Hans was the gentle one.
Margarete,
with her red hair and artist's spunk,
was never afraid to speak her mind.
Like Hans,
she enjoyed animals and zoos and the circus.
Together, they made a great team.

1935

That August,
Hans and Margarete were married
and they lived together in their Rio apartment
with two pet marmosets.
Those little monkeys were *always* getting into mischief.
During this time,
Margarete decided to shorten her name to Margret.

Reyersbach . . .
Reyersbach . . .
It was a hard name for Brazilians to pronounce.
Now that Hans was trying to earn money
by drawing and painting large posters and maps,
he began to sign his work
"H. A. Rey."
It was much easier for clients in his new country.
And . . .
it was a name to remember.

Opposite, photograph: *Adolf Hitler marching with Nazi officials in Berlin, ca. 1933*
Opposite, bottom right: *Business card drawn by H.A. Rey*
Top: *Poster by H. A. Rey*

A Hotel in Paris

Months later,
as Brazilian citizens with Brazilian passports,
the Reys began a honeymoon trip to Europe
and took their Rio pets with them.
It was a cold rainy crossing to England.
Margret knitted sweaters
to keep the tiny monkeys warm, but, even so,
the marmosets didn't survive the journey.

After visiting several cities,
Hans and Margret ended up at the

Terrass Hotel
12, rue Joseph de Maistre
Paris.

Above: *From Curious George, 1941*
Opposite, from top: *From Curious George, 1941;*
from Katy No-Pocket, *1944*

The Reys planned to stay at this hotel for two weeks
because it was in Montmartre,
the neighborhood of Paris that was famous
for the many artists who had lived there.
Beautiful Paris was elegant and exciting.
It seemed to be just the right city for Hans and Margret,
so the Terrass Hotel became their home
for the next four years.

The Terrass had two large buildings,
one with guest rooms and one with apartments.

The Reys took an apartment on the fifth floor,
number 505.
Pets were allowed at the hotel,
so for a few years
Hans and Margret had two French turtles
to keep them company:
Claudia and Claudius.

In every season,
Hans and Margret looked across the rooftops and chimney pots.
What a view!
They never grew tired of seeing the graceful Eiffel Tower
etched against the blue or gray Paris sky.

Top: *Paris photograph of H.A. Rey taken by Margret Rey*
Bottom: *The Eiffel Tower, 1930s*

From their windows in 505,
the Reys could hear the flutter of pigeons
on the balcony ledge
and, down below,
the quick rumble of taxis on the rue de Maistre.
Just across the street in the cemetery
was a spooky jumble of vaults, graves, and tombstones,
dark with the soot of the city.

The Reys' neighborhood,
Montmartre,
was really an old village on the highest hill of the city,
with vineyards,
stray cats,
and the windmill of the famed Moulin Rouge cabaret.

Steep cobblestone streets
wound up,
and up,
and up to Sacre Coeur,
a landmark church with gleaming white domes.

The Reys sketched and photographed
the fishermen along the banks of the Seine . . .
the captains and their families who lived on the local barges . . .
the booksellers on the quays who, each morning,
unlocked their wooden boxes
and sold secondhand books to those who passed by . . .
and, of course, the animals at the zoo.

Often,
Hans and Margret walked to their favorite cafés for lunch or dinner.
They sat at sidewalk tables with their friends,
drank cups of strong coffee,
and talked about their creative ideas
as they watched the world move by.

Four Paris photographs taken by Margret Rey, 1939–40

Books for Children

During these years,
Hans and Margret began writing and illustrating
their books for children.
Margret was a good critic for Hans's drawings.

The Reys worked with several publishers in Paris,
and another one in London.
They exchanged detailed letters with their editors
about their new projects.

Above left and right: Interior art from Cecily G. and the 9 Monkeys

Right: *Letters from the Reys' British and French publishers*

The years were carefully recorded by Hans.
Each day,
he jotted down the places he and Margret visited,
living expenses,
and notes about his work.
He filled page after page of his pocket calendar
with his small, penciled script,
writing words in French, English, and German.
Then he added up the monthly expenses in French francs.

In 1939,
a wonderful new manuscript was in progress:
a story about a monkey named Fifi
who had appeared in one of Hans's first books.
Now Fifi would be the star of his own book,
The Adventures of Fifi.
Fifi was a very *curious* little monkey—
he was always getting into trouble
and then finding a way to get out of it.

1

This is the story about Fifi
who lived in the djungle somewhere in Africa.
He was very happy and he was a good little monkey.
He only had one fault:
he was very curious
and always tried to imitate everything.

Counterclockwise from top left: *H. A. Rey's 1936 diary;*
early manuscript page; H. A. Rey's diary page from June 1938

1939

War Begins

On September 1, 1939,
war began in Europe.
The battles were far away—in Poland.
Still, many Parisians left the city
until times seemed more secure.
That week,
Margret and Hans packed their valises
and took a long train ride southwest
to a remote village in the French countryside.
They spent the next four months
at Château Feuga,
with its walls and towers
that were more than five hundred years old.

German invasion of Poland, September 1939
Inset: *Photograph of Château Feuga taken in 1939*
by Margret Rey Opposite: From Whiteblack the Penguin, 2000

Up . . . up . . .
round and round . . .
Hans climbed the creaky, narrow stairs
to a square room
in the largest of Feuga's three towers.
He pushed open the heavy shutters
and smelled the fresh September air.
Far to the south was a
smudge of mountains:
the Pyrenées!

This simple room was the
perfect place for a studio
where Hans could work
on his book illustrations.
Or read, or sit at his desk
and think and daydream as
he often liked to do.

From Château Feuga
it was an hour's walk to the closest post office,
but still the Reys wrote and mailed letters to their publishers.
Besides *The Adventures of Fifi,*
Hans and Margret began working on another book—
this one about a penguin named Whiteblack,
who loved to travel and see the world.

But since September
France had been at war with Germany,
and the Reys had German accents when they spoke French.
A few local people whispered among themselves
and called the village police officer,
who then paid a visit to Feuga.
Were these château guests perhaps German spies?

Hans led the officer up the stairs to his studio.
The scattered pages of sketches and words,
and watercolor illustrations of Fifi, the little monkey,
and Whiteblack, the penguin,
told the true story:
Hans and Margret created books for children.

Top: *German troops marching to the Polish front, 1939*
Middle: *Two illustrations from Curious George, 1941*
26   Bottom right: *From Whiteblack the Penguin, 2000*

In 1939,
Hitler's Germany was not a safe place for Jewish
people to live.
Hans and Margret worried about old friends
still living in Hamburg.
Their own families had moved away
to London or Rio,
and the Reys were glad to be living in France,
glad they had become Brazilian citizens
while in South America.
Brazil was a neutral country
in the brewing conflict in Europe.

In December,
it was cold and drafty in the tower studio,
too cold to open the shutters.
There was snow on the peaks of the Pyrenées.
Hans carried his artwork downstairs,
and he and Margret packed up their belongings.
The war was still far away,
not yet in France.
It was safe to return home to the Terrass.

Left: *Card made for Margret Rey by H. A. Rey, December 24, 1939*
Right: *From Whiteblack the Penguin, 2000*

The Winter of 1940

*T*hat January the Reys were back in Paris.
The streets and cafés seemed bustling and noisy
after the quiet months at Feuga.
But Hans and Margret loved the energy of the city.
Hans completed the title page for *The Adventures of Fifi*:
a picture of Fifi in a tree at the zoo,
holding the string of a red balloon.
Then he signed the illustration in small black letters:

H.a.Rey-Paris Jan. 1940

Hans was also hard at work in 505
painting the watercolors for *Whiteblack the Penguin*.
One morning
he dipped his brush into some black paint.
In two of the illustrations
Hans lettered the name *PEGGY*, his nickname for Margret,
on a fishing boat.
After all,
the Reys were a team.

1940

Top left: *Original title page of Curious George, 1941*
Bottom right: *From Whiteblack the Penguin, 2000*

On his tiny calendar,

Hans recorded the work days as they slipped by:

Penguin . . .

Penguin . . .

Penguin . . .

He studied the illustrations of this new story. *Hmm.*

He liked them as much as those for *The Adventures of Fifi.*

Perhaps . . . even better.

Hans carefully painted a tiny French flag

on the stern of Whiteblack's ship.

The Reys hoped to go on a ship soon themselves,

to America for a visit in April.

But it was difficult to leave Europe now

because of wartime regulations.

Top: *From Whiteblack the Penguin, 2000*

Bottom: *H. A. Rey's diary pages from January 1940*

Margret's older brother, also named Hans,
came to Paris that winter for a visit.
The winter of 1940 was the coldest anyone could remember.
Now there was snow on the balcony ledge
and on the high walls of the cemetery.
Hans Rey the artist and Hans Waldstein,
a soldier in the French army,
stood together in the cold sunshine
on the roof garden of the Terrass
while Margret snapped their pictures.

Photographs taken by Margret Rey, 1940

Working by the Sea

During the windy days of March,
Hans worked hard on some final touches for *Fifi*.
Then, in April,
the Reys packed their suitcases
for a train trip to Avranches,
a town on the far edge of Normandy,
on the English Channel.
Now Hans and Margret could enjoy the sea air
and look across the wide bay
to the ancient fortress Mont St. Michel,
a castle built on a rock in the shallow tidal flats.

Would *Fifi* and *Whiteblack* ever become published books?
Because of the war, there were now strict laws about printing.
Typesetters had joined the army.
Paper was getting scarce.
Hans mailed letters to editors in London and Paris
and included the Reys' vacation address.

H. A. Rey
Hotel D`Angleterre
Avranches (Manche)

The Reys were relieved when Hans signed a contract
for *Fifi*, as well as for two small manuscripts,
and received an advance of money from their Paris publisher.
Little did they know how needed those French francs would be
in the weeks to follow.

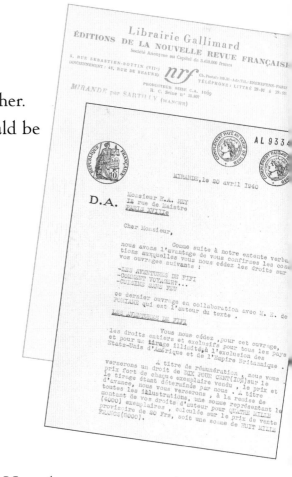

Margret and Hans began a new project:
a book of nursery songs in French and English.
Hans drew the strong black lines of his style
and added the musical notes.
In wartime, children needed
good books and songs more than ever.

Opposite, left: *Editorial letter from the Reys' British publisher*
Opposite, background: *Mont-Saint-Michel*
Top right: *H. A. Rey's contract with French publisher Gallimard*
Middle and bottom: *Two pages from H. A. Rey's Au Claire de la
Lune and Other French Nursery Songs, 1941*

The Terrible Week

On the morning of May 10, 1940,
while Hans was again at his desk,
touching up a page of *Fifi,*
history was happening.

Miles away from Avranches,
the German army crossed over the border
into the neutral countries of Holland and Belgium.

That day Hans bought two local newspapers.
In the cafés, people listened intently
to the radio broadcasts of the rapid German advance.
Everyone was worried.
Some had sons or brothers fighting with the French army.

But . . .
the French army was strong!
It was mighty!
It would protect Avranches . . .
and all of France!
It would stop the advance of the Germans.

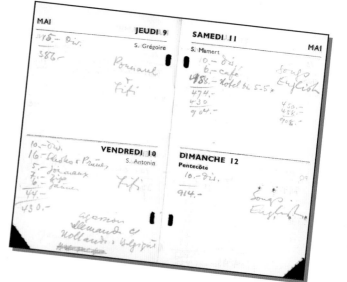

Top: *Dutch street in May 1940*
Bottom and above right: *H. A. Rey's diary pages from May 1940*
Opposite: *German troops in France, ca. 1940–1945*

That terrible week,

it was hard for Hans and Margret to put their hearts into their work.

France was their home now.

On May 13,

Hans wrote in his diary:

Songs English

very slowly because of the events.

The war was no longer far away.

On the northern French border,

the Nazi tanks moved like lightning.

It was a *blitzkrieg!*

On May 19, Hans recorded *Songs* in his notebook.

It would be the last day that H. A. Rey

painted his book illustrations in France.

From then on,

he and Margret needed to focus on their safety

in the time of war.

They bought train tickets to return home.

ESCAPE FROM PARIS

◆

PART II

Paris in Wartime

On May 23,
the Reys arrived back in Paris
and took the metro to Montmartre.
The cafés were still open and busy,
but the tempo of the city had changed.

From the north came a stream of refugees—
more and more arrived in Paris each day.
Hundreds . . . then thousands . . .
then thousands more.
Train stations were filled with people.
Such anxious faces and so few trains!
Everyone wanted to travel in the same direction:
south . . . away from the fighting.
There was not enough food or water at the stations.
In the unusual June heat,
some refugees fainted.
The elegant avenues of the French capital
were crowded with bicycles,
Belgian farm carts and horses,
and Dutch cars with mattresses strapped to the roof.
All belonged to civilians fleeing from the war zones to the north.
Even barges on the Seine carried refugees.
The stories in the Paris newspapers were full of gloomy news.

Plans to Flee

At their Terrass apartment,
Hans and Margret remained calm.
But they were German-born Jews,
and Hitler's soldiers were moving swiftly
toward the French capital.
The Reys would have to leave, and quickly.

They decided to try to return to Brazil,
and then travel on to America.
Margret's sister was there,
near New York City.

But there was much to do before they could leave.
One needed *so many papers* to leave a country in a time of war.
Identity cards.
Visas.
And tickets.
Tickets for any trains heading south.
And *money!*
One always needed money for a long journey . . .
Would they get it all in time?

The next day,

Hans went immediately to the Brazilian consulate

and paid for updated passports.

He withdrew money from his bank accounts,

as many francs as he was allowed.

That week,

the Reys went to the same few places

over and over again to get the documents

they needed for their journey:

the American consulate . . .

the Portuguese consulate . . .

the Spanish consulate . . .

and again, the bank.

Then back to the consulates.

Everywhere they went for their documents,

there were long queues that wound around street corners.

Thump-thump! Thump-thump!

Everything needed to be official.

Everything needed to be stamped with the date.

The list of expenses in Hans's notebook grew and grew:

baggage . . .

        insurance . . .

              taxi . . .

                    tailor . . .

                  umbrella . . .

Hans's calendar became a record of a husband and wife,

two artists,

getting ready to leave their beloved home.

Opposite, top: *H.A. Rey's Brazilian passport*
Opposite, bottom: *Pages from the Reys' French identity cards*
Right: *H. A. Rey's diary pages from May 1940*

At night,
the streets of Paris had an eerie dark blue gleam
from the blackout cloth on the streetlamps.
The slow, loud whine of air raid sirens,
mostly false alarms,
woke the city night after night.

The news from the front was grim.
The Belgian king had surrendered to the Germans.
Most of the British army,
and more than 100,000 French soldiers,
had to be rescued from the beaches at Dunkirk.
The English Channel was full of hundreds of boats and ships
trying to save the retreating armies,
taking them to safety in England.

On June 7,
Hans recorded in his notebook
that the neighborhood was awakened in the night
by an alert from the *préfecture*.

By June 10,
two million Parisians had left the city,
including the government officials
who fled first to Tours,
and then farther south to Bordeaux.
Only one newspaper was still being printed in Paris.
Monuments and historic buildings were ringed with sandbags
as protection against bombs and fighting.
Shops were shuttered.
Taxis were impossible to find.

A belated radio broadcast let citizens know
that Paris had been declared an open city.
The government had decided not to barricade its streets
or fight the invading army,
whose tanks could turn the French capital into rubble in a matter of days.
Major avenues and the lovely, wide Champs-Élysées were empty.
Paris was waiting . . .

A BICYCLE MAKER

*H*ans and Margret were among the few tenants
still at the Terrass Hotel.
On June 11,
the Reys went scouting for two bicycles to buy
since they had no car,
and the trains were no longer running.
They found a small shop open,
but the owner shrugged and pointed to a tandem *vélo*.
It was the only bicycle left in his store.
"You should have come sooner, monsieur."
Hans wheeled the long bicycle outside
and persuaded Margret to practice riding it with him
on the rue de la Paix
and around the Place Vendôme.
It was a disaster!
Margret shook her head
and said that riding a tandem would *never* work.

VELO Bicyclette

Let's go!

Ready?

Ring.
Ring!

The Reys returned the bicycle and bargained with the owner.
For 1,600 francs, almost a month's lodging at the Terrass,
Hans bought spare parts for two bicycles
from the shelves of the *vélo* store,
and four large baskets.
Margret hurried back to their apartment
and chose a small pile of belongings.
She took the Reys' manuscripts and artwork from the desk
and slid them carefully into a satchel.

Meanwhile,
Hans worked in the back room of the store,
with tools, handlebars, pedals, and tires.
With baskets on each bicycle,
the Reys would be able to pack a few more things for their journey.
Then Hans recorded his work in his pocket calendar.
That hot June afternoon,
H. A. Rey, the artist,
became a bicycle maker.

The biggest adventure of his life was about to begin . . .

PEDALING SOUTH

On Wednesday, June 12,
it was raining on the empty streets of Paris.
Finally raining,
after the days of hot weather.
At five-thirty in the morning,
the Reys began their flight from the city,
across wet cobblestone streets
that glistened beneath their tires.

The Reys had to travel light:
only a few clothes and their winter coats,
some bread and cheese,
a little meat, water,
an umbrella,
Hans's pipe,
and the precious manuscripts,
including *The Adventures of Fifi.*

Everything else they owned was left behind.
Hans hoped the boxes and suitcases at the Terrass
would somehow be shipped safely
to Margret's sister in America as planned.

Hans and Margret joined the thousands of refugees leaving Paris.
After the first kilometers, the Reys' clothes were damp with rain
so Hans made sure that his artwork
stayed dry in the basket under his winter coat.
Hans and Margret rode in and out of the lines of cars,
taxis and trucks,
green city buses and farm carts,
other bicycles and stragglers on foot.

The drizzle of rain stopped and the sun came out.
The Reys pedaled . . . and pedaled . . . and pedaled.
With each kilometer,
the seats of their *vélos*
felt harder on their backsides.
Their necks and their backs began to ache.
And their legs and their knees.
Even the palms of their hands.

Everywhere
there was confusion and noise:
grinding gears of overheated cars
and the frightening drone of German scout planes.
Constant and relentless were the car horns,
honking to speed up the crawling procession
of the largest motorized evacuation in history.

More than five million people were on the roads of France that day.
Among this sea of humanity were two small figures:
Margret and H. A. Rey.

Help Along the Way

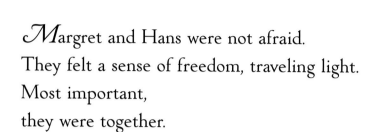

$\mathcal{M}$argret and Hans were not afraid.
They felt a sense of freedom, traveling light.
Most important,
they were together.

That first day,
the Reys pedaled forty-eight kilometers to the town of Étampes.
Past the crowded main square,
they found a farmhouse set back from the road.
The owner offered Margret and Hans simple lodging:
a room already housing a servant and a woman refugee.
The grateful Reys wrapped themselves in their coats
and instantly fell asleep.

By three o'clock the next morning,
Margret and Hans were on their way again in the darkness.
The sky was a blue-black canvas filled with stars.
As the sun rose,
the road flattened out into open land.
That day, Hans and Margret pedaled twenty-six kilometers
until they reached the tiny village of Acquebouille.

They spied a farm on a side road
and walked their bicycles into a walled yard full of thick mud
and clucking hens.
Once again,
the Reys were lucky.
A kindly farmwoman offered them sweet, fresh milk
as well as a place to sleep.
Hans recorded the route and events:
Nuit au etable aux vaches..
That night,
Hans and Margret Rey slept on a bed of hay
in a stable full of cows.

Above: H. A. Rey's June 1940 diary pages, written in French

Early the next day,
the Reys were off again,
pedaling,
pedaling,
thirty-two kilometers from Acquebouille to the city of Orléans.
There Hans and Margret hoped to catch a train
that would take them south.
They still had far to go:
their destination was Portugal . . .
and then . . .
a ship across the Atlantic.

The train station in Orléans was bedlam!
There were a few hand-lettered signs for missing children,
tacked up on the walls by frantic parents:

Jean-Claude Moncourt, 5 ans, perdu le 10 juin.
Helene et Martine Landau . . . 6 et 4 ans—perdu pres d'ici le 11 juin.

These were difficult days for the French people.

Two days after the Reys passed through,
Étampes was heavily bombed.
Their escape had been narrow indeed.

At the Orléans station,
Hans touched his inside pocket
checking that the documents
and tickets he had bought in Paris
were safe.
Then he and Margret hoisted their bicycles
and dusty bundles into the crowded train car
headed in the direction of Bordeaux.
The train slowly pulled out of the Orléans station,
then swayed and clattered along the tracks
as it gathered speed.

To Hans and Margret,
after three days of pedaling,
the sound was wonderful.

The date was Friday, June 14, 1940,
a terrible day in the history of Paris:

Nazi troops had goose-stepped by the thousands
down the broad Champs-Élysées
and replaced the French flag flying atop the Eiffel Tower
with the swastika of Hitler's Third Reich.

Occupied Paris was only 106 kilometers to the north.
Safety for the Reys lay in the long journey ahead.
Margret and Hans dozed and talked
as they watched two days and two nights
cover the landscape.
Hans jotted down the direction of their route in his diary
as he sat with Margret by the open windows hour after hour.
The air was hot inside the train.
What had happened to Paris and the Terrass Hotel?
Were their other friends safe?
So many questions without answers.

WEARY REFUGEES

*F*inally,
close to five A.M. on June 16,
the Reys' train pulled into the station at Bayonne.
Hans and Margret,
tired and disheveled,
climbed down to the platform
and pushed their bicycles through the crowds of people,
inhaling the air of southern France.
What a clamor of station noise!
But what a relief!

The population of the small town was triple its usual size.
Local police pointed them in the direction of the public high school.
That night,
after being welcomed with plates of good food,
Hans and Margret curled up again on their winter coats,
surrounded by hundreds of other weary refugees.

The next morning,
Hans counted up their remaining francs.
The amount was shrinking, day by day.
The Reys bought only a few things:
soap,
shirts,
two jackets,
a shawl,
and a backpack.
Hans sent telegrams to London and Rio,
telling family and friends that they had gotten out of Paris.

The Reys left Bayonne
and bicycled down the coast to nearby Biarritz
to get more travel visas.
Outside the Portuguese consulate
in the shade of the tamarind trees,
Hans and Margret waited in line for four hours.
Those who couldn't get permission to travel through Spain or Portugal
would have to remain in occupied France for the duration of the war.

Finally,
Margret and Hans were granted their transit visas.
Thump! Thump!
They would be allowed to travel on to Hendaye,
the French border town a few kilometers south.
There they would need approval to board the train for Spain.
Others,
ahead of them and behind them in line,
were not so fortunate.

That night, in Hendaye,
the Reys spread out their coats on the floor of a small restaurant.
With a handful of francs,
they had persuaded a waiter
to let them spend the night there.

The next morning,
at the Spanish consulate,
their wait was five hours.
Then . . . finally . . .
a weary Spanish official stamped the Reys' papers.
Margret and Hans celebrated by eating a lunch of sardines and tuna fish.
Now they could travel through Spain
and on to Portugal.

And the two bicycles
that had carried the Reys
all those kilometers out of Paris?
Hans sold them on the train platform
to a customs official for 650 francs.
The Reys would not be needing them in Lisbon,
or onboard a ship to America.

ACROSS SPAIN

The train from Hendaye
was so overcrowded with Polish émigrés
that Margret and Hans had to stand in the swaying car
before they could find seats.
An official passed slowly through their car,
checking identity papers with stern eyes.
He began to question Hans about his job
and asked Hans to open up his leather satchel.
Perhaps these passengers were spies,
leaving France with important papers?

Then the official thumbed through the pages of *The Adventures of Fifi*.
"Ah . . . *un livre pour les enfants.*"

The official smiled briefly.
He handed the passports and visas back to Hans
and moved on.
Once again,
the mischievious little monkey had rescued the Reys.

Hans and Margret Rey had been on the run for nine days.
For two more days,
the train chugged across Spain,
past olive groves and open plains
to the border town of Fuentes de Oñoro.

During the long customs check,
Hans was glad that he still had some money in his pocket
when the local clerks demanded inflated fees in pesetas.
Finally the train crossed into Portugal.

WAITING IN LISBON

On Sunday, June 23, at one-thirty in the afternoon,
Margret and Hans Rey arrived in Lisbon.
The neutral capital had suddenly become "the city of refugees."
Lisbon was now the safe haven for diplomats,
and a temporary destination for thousands of others
who were trying to leave Europe on one of the ships in the harbor.

Somehow,
despite the crowds,
the Reys found a hotel room.
A real bed . . .
with pillows and clean sheets.
And a bathtub with hot water.
"Wonderful! And much too good!"
Hans wrote in his pocket diary.
Both of the Reys were asleep before nine that night.

Right away the next morning they made phone calls,
wrote letters to family and friends,
and sent a telegram
to their bank in Rio:

have had a very narrow escape
Baggage all lost
have not sufficient money in hand

While waiting for passage on a ship,
the Reys' address for the next month
was a few blocks from the straw-colored Tagus River:
Rua do Ferregial de Baixo 33.

After money was wired to their bank in Lisbon,
Hans and Margret were able to shop for pajamas
and other essential things,
as well as paper and paints.

The two artists were safe in neutral Portugal,
but other parts of France, in addition to Paris,
were now under the dark shadow of German occupation.
For many Europeans,
the war years of terror and fear were just beginning.

On July 15,
Margret and Hans had their required vaccination papers
signed and stamped.
Once again they began to pack their belongings.
Far across the Atlantic was Rio . . .
their next steppingstone to a new life in America.

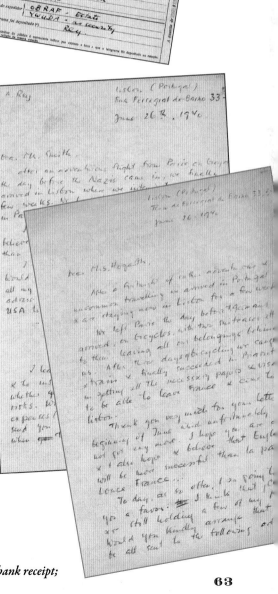

Opposite: *H. A. Rey's June 21, 1940, diary page, written in French and German*
Clockwise from top left: *Telegram sent by H.A. Rey from Lisbon; visa stamp, July 15, 1940; bank receipt; letters to editors written by the Reys from Lisbon*

An Ocean Voyage

On July 21,
Hans and Margret walked up the gangplank of the *Angola*,
carrying their luggage and first-class tickets
for a thirteen-day passage to South America.

The wide bow of the *Angola*
cut through the dark blue swells of the Atlantic
as the steamship, crowded with refugees,
headed out to sea.
It docked briefly at Vicente, a town on the Portuguese island of Madeira,
and then sailed southwest toward Rio.

Each morning,
the Reys could see the sun come up over the ocean
from the small porthole in their stateroom.

Almost all of the passengers on the *Angola*
had fled from their homes because of the war.
All had stories to tell
at their tables in the dining room.
When the *Angola* rolled and pitched in rough weather,
the plates and silverware slid sideways with a clatter.

64

Lisbon

Vicente, Madeira

Rio de Janeiro

Brazil

New ideas

WAITING IN RIO

On August 4,
the *Angola* cruised slowly along the coast of Brazil
and into Rio de Janeiro's wide harbor.

Once again,
the Reys had to find lodging
as they waited for passage to America on another ship.
Their new address was

    Caixa 116
    Rio de Janeiro
    Brasil

They called up old Brazilian friends,
and they worried about those left behind in wartime Europe.
Some of the letters they wrote to their families and editors
took many weeks to arrive.
Others were never received.

On October 3,
after two months of waiting,
Hans and Margret boarded a Brazilian ship in Rio's sunny harbor
to begin the last leg of their unexpected journey.

One clear night,
they took a late evening stroll on the windy deck.
What bright stars!
The ocean sky was like a huge blackboard
dotted with tiny lights.
All Hans needed was a stick of celestial chalk
to connect these Atlantic stars
and map his favorite constellations.

A New Home

On October 14, 1940,
four months after they bicycled out of Paris,
the Reys saw the New York City skyline
framed by a blue sky and brilliant sunshine.
Their ship followed the wake of a sturdy tugboat
into New York Harbor.
Passengers began to point and cheer.
There, ahead,
was the Statue of Liberty,
the landmark of freedom
given to America in friendship
by the country of France.

Margret and Hans leaned against the ship railing
and pulled up their collars,
facing the cold, steady breeze.
An unknown future in the United States
lay ahead for the two artists.

Like Fifi,
the mischievous monkey whose book of adventures
they had carried in a bicycle basket,
Hans and Margret Rey had had a narrow escape
from wartime Paris.
But the Reys had talent
and enough energy to climb mountains if they had to,
in creating new books.

That chilly October day in New York Harbor,
Hans, Margret, and Fifi were on their way . . .
to a new home,
on another continent,
with stories to tell.

Just a year later,
their first book would be published in America,
a book that would bring all three of them
enduring fame and affection throughout the world.
Like Hans Reyersbach and Margarete Waldstein,
the little French monkey Fifi would change his name,
and it would become one to remember . . .
the well-loved Curious George.

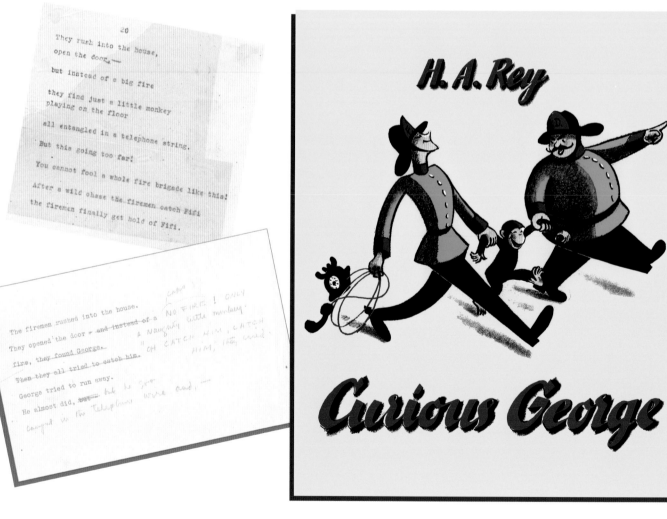

Top: *Interior art from Curious George, 1941, and cover art, below*
Left: *Draft of Curious George*

After the Escape

*P*aris remained occupied by German troops until its liberation on August 25, 1944. Nine months after arriving in the United States in October 1940, the Reys received the belongings they had packed up in Paris, including their publishing contracts and correspondence. No one knows how their luggage was shipped from France.

Margret and Hans lived for the next twenty-three years in New York City. They led modest lives, surrounded by books and their pet cocker spaniels. In November 1940, a new editor at Houghton Mifflin, Grace Hogarth, offered the Reys a contract for four books. The Reys had known Grace when she was a children's book editor at their British publisher, Chatto and Windus. Like Margret and Hans, she had also left Europe because of the wartime dangers. The contract included the manuscripts for *The Adventures of Fifi* (eventually retitled *Curious George*), *Raffy and the 9 Monkeys* (retitled *Cecily G. and the 9 Monkeys*), and two lift-the-flap books, *How Do You Get There?* and *Anybody at Home?* Margret and Hans carried all of these with them when they biked out of Paris.

Curious George was published in the fall of 1941. It has sold over twenty-seven million copies and been translated into more than fourteen languages. The book of nursery songs that the Reys worked on while in Avranches was published in 1941 by Greystone Press. It was displayed in a bookstore window on New York's Fifth Avenue to celebrate the hope for international peace. *Whiteblack the Penguin* wasn't published until 2000, when Anita Silvey, who was then publisher of Houghton Mifflin Children's Books, rediscovered it in the Rey archives.

On April 8, 1946, Margret and Hans Rey became United States citizens. In later years, the Reys built a summer home in Waterville Valley, New Hampshire, where Hans set up his telescope to view the stars and night skies. In 1963 they moved from New York to Cambridge, Massachusetts. Margret and Hans had no children of their own, but their pictures and words have brought joy to millions of young readers around the world.

H. A. Rey died in Boston on August 26, 1977, at the age of seventy-eight. His beloved "Peggy," cared for by a trusted friend, Lay Lee Ong, lived to celebrate her ninetieth birthday. Until her death on December 21, 1996, in Cambridge, Margret continued to be a strong voice and guardian for the Reys' texts and illustrations, and for the mischievous monkey George. In this new century, the humor and truth in their books continue to charm and inspire us.

A Partial Bibliography of Books by Margret and H. A. Rey

BOOKS BY H. A. REY

Zebrology. London: Chatto & Windus, 1937.

Le Cirque. Paris: Hachette, 1938.

Le Zoo. Paris: Hachette, 1938.

Rafi et les 9 singes. Paris: Gallimard (NRF), [1939].

Raffy and the 9 Monkeys. London: Chatto & Windus, 1939.

Anybody at Home? London: Chatto & Windus, 1939.

Au Clair de la Lune and Other French Nursery Songs. New York: Greystone Press, 1941.

Curious George. Boston: Houghton Mifflin, 1941.

How Do You Get There? Boston: Houghton Mifflin, 1941.

Cecily G. and the 9 Monkeys. Boston: Houghton Mifflin, 1942.

A Christmas Manger: A New Kind of Punch-Out-and-Play Book. Boston: Houghton Mifflin, 1942.

Elizabite: Adventures of a Carnivorous Plant. New York & London: Harper & Brothers, 1942; Houghton Mifflin, 1999.

Uncle Gus's Circus: A New Kind of Cut-Out-and-Play Book. Boston: Houghton Mifflin, 1942.

Uncle Gus's Farm: A New Kind of Cut-Out-and-Play Book. Boston: Houghton Mifflin, 1942.

Tommy Helps, Too. Boston: Houghton Mifflin, 1943.

Where's My Baby? Boston: Houghton Mifflin, 1943.

Feed the Animals. Boston: Houghton Mifflin, 1944.

Curious George Takes a Job. Boston: Houghton Mifflin, 1947.

Curious George Rides a Bike. Boston: Houghton Mifflin, 1952.

The Stars: A New Way to See Them. Boston: Houghton Mifflin, 1952.

Find the Constellations. Boston: Houghton Mifflin, 1954.

See the Circus. Boston: Houghton Mifflin, 1956.

Curious George Gets a Medal. Boston: Houghton Mifflin, 1957.

Curious George Learns the Alphabet. Boston: Houghton Mifflin, 1963.

The Original Curious George. Boston: Houghton Mifflin, 1998.

BOOKS BY MARGRET AND H. A. REY

How the Flying Fishes Came into Being. London: Chatto & Windus, 1938.

Pretzel. Boston: Houghton Mifflin, 1944.

Spotty. Boston: Houghton Mifflin, 1945.

Curious George Flies a Kite. Boston: Houghton Mifflin, 1958.

Curious George Goes to the Hospital. Boston: Houghton Mifflin, 1966.

The Complete Adventures of Curious George. Introduction by Madeline L'Engle. Afterword by Margret Rey. Boston: Houghton Mifflin, 1994.

Whiteblack the Penguin Sees the World. Boston: Houghton Mifflin, 2000.

The Complete Adventures of Curious George. Introduction by Leonard S. Marcus. Retrospective Essay by Dee Jones. Boston: Houghton Mifflin, 2001.

Curious George and Friends: Favorite Stories. Introduction by Margaret Bloy Graham. Boston: Houghton Mifflin, 2003.

Billy's Picture. New York: Harper & Brothers, 1948; Boston: Houghton Mifflin, 2004.

BOOKS ILLUSTRATED BY H. A. REY

The Park Book by Charlotte Zolotow. New York: Harper Books, 1944.

Katy No-Pocket by Emmy Payne. Boston: Houghton Mifflin, 1944.

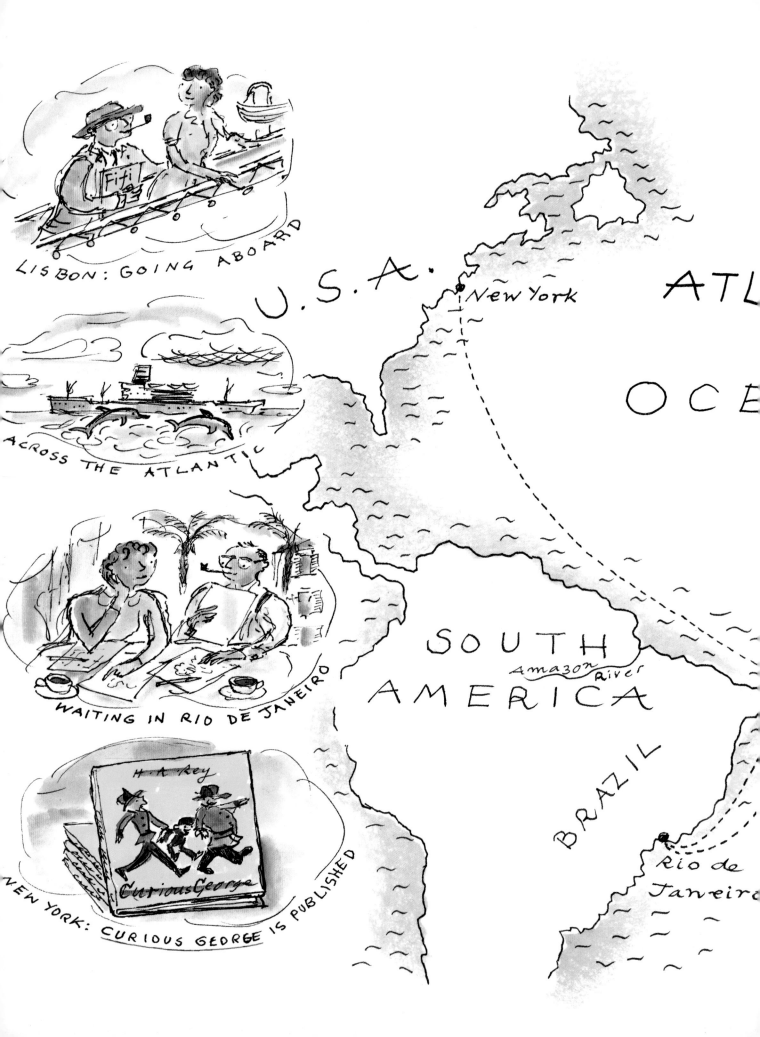

LISBON: GOING ABOARD

ACROSS THE ATLANTIC

WAITING IN RIO DE JANEIRO

NEW YORK: CURIOUS GEORGE IS PUBLISHED

U.S.A.

New York

ATL

OCE

SOUTH
AMERICA

Amazon River

BRAZIL

Rio de Janeiro

Picture Credits

Library of Congress, Prints & Photographs Division, Photochrom Collection:
Pages 6 (foreground left: LC-DIG-ppmsca-00415; foreground right: LC-CIG-ppmsca-00424; background: LC-DIG-ppmsca-00419), 8 (LC-DIG-ppmsca-00404), 32 (background: LC-DIG-ppmsc-05136)

H. A. & Margret Rey, Papers, de Grummond Children's Literature Collection, The University of Southern Mississippi: title page (right), pages 1 (right), 4, 5, (both), 7 (bottom), 9 (all), 10, 11 (top and middle), 12 (middle and bottom right), 14 (foreground), 15, 18, (top), 20-21 (all), 22 (letters), 23 (top, bottom left and right), 24 (foreground), 27 (bottom), 29 (bottom), 30-31 (all), 32 (left), 33 (top right), 34 (bottom), 35 (top), 40 (both), 41 (bottom), 51 (inset), 62 (inset), 63 (all except label), 64, 70 (left)

Bettman/CORBIS: pages 24 (background), 34 (top)

Hulton-Deutsch Collection/CORBIS: pages 18 (bottom), 26 (top)

Underwood and Underwood/CORBIS: pages 14 (background and top right)

CORBIS: page 35 (bottom)

© 2003 me & my BIG ideas™: labels on pages 14, 18, 22, 32, 63

⤨

Illustrations from *Cecily G. and the 9 Monkeys* by H. A. Rey. Copyright 1942, and Copyright © renewed 1969 by H. A. Rey. Reprinted by permission of Houghton Mifflin Company. All rights reserved.

Illustrations from *Curious George* by H. A. Rey. Copyright 1941, and copyright © renewed 1969 by Margret E. Rey. Copyright assigned to Houghton Mifflin Company in 1993. Reprinted by permission of Houghton Mifflin Company. All rights reserved.

Illustrations by H. A. Rey from *Katy No-Pocket* by Emmy Payne. Copyright 1944 by Houghton Mifflin Company. Copyright © renewed 1972 by Emmy Govan West. Reprinted by permission of Houghton Mifflin Company. All rights reserved.

Illustrations from *Whiteblack the Penguin Sees the World* by Margret and H. A. Rey. Copyright © 2000 by Lay Lee Ong. Reprinted by permission of the Rey Estate.

Au Claire de la Lune and Other French Nursery Songs, Copyright © 1941 by H. A. Rey, Greystone Press. Copyright © renewed 1991 by the Rey Estate. Reprinted by permission of the Rey Estate.

⤨

The text of this book is set in Pastonch and Freestyle.
The illustrations are watercolor on paper.

⤨

The Library of Congress has cataloged the hardcover edition as follows:
Borden, Louise.
    The journey that saved Curious George : the true wartime escape of Margret and H. A. Rey / by Louise Borden ; illustrated by Allan Drummond.
        p. cm.
    ISBN 978-0-618-33924-2 hardcover
    ISBN 978-0-547-41746-2 paperback
    1. Rey, Margret—Juvenile literature. 2. Rey, H. A. (Hans Augusto), 1898—Juvenile literature. 3. Authors, American—20th century—Biography—Juvenile literature. 4. Refugees, Jewish—United States—Biography—Juvenile literature. 5. Jewish authors—united States—Biography—Juvenile literature. 6. curious George (Fictitious character)—Juvenile literature. 7. Children's stories—Authorship—Juvenile literature. I. Title.
    PS3535.E924Z623 2005
    813'.52—dc22   2004001015
Manufactured in China
LEO 10 9 8 7 6 5 4 3 2 1
4500218359